YOU DIDN'T FIND THIS JOURNAL BY ACCIDENT.

LUMISEA PRESS

First Edition: 2025
ISBN: 978-1-966544-02-9
Published by LumiSea Press San Diego, CA
Printed in the United States of America

Welcome to LIVE WIRE!

You're holding more than a journal — this is a mirror for your energy, a record of who you're becoming, and a spark to keep your inner current alive. Over the next 90 days, you'll track what lights you up, what drains you, and what calls you forward. Each page is an invitation to connect more deeply with yourself — to listen, to notice, and to remember your own brilliance.

By the end, you'll have something rare: a living map of your personal electricity — your courage, your clarity, and the choices that make you feel most alive.

LET'S GET STARTED...

A NOTE ON PAPER QUALITY

THIS EDITION OF LIVE WIRE IS PRINTED THROUGH
AMAZON'S STANDARD PROCESS (THE ONLY OPTION),
WHICH MEANS THE PAGES ARE ON THE LIGHTER SIDE.
THEY WORK BEAUTIFULLY WITH
PENS, PENCILS, OR FINE-TIP MARKERS—
BUT HEAVIER INKS OR ALCOHOL-BASED MARKERS
MAY BLEED THROUGH.
IF YOU LOVE BOLD TOOLS,
JUST SLIP A SHEET OF PAPER BEHIND THE PAGE
FOR PROTECTION.

A PREMIUM COLOR VERSION
PRINTED ON THICKER, HIGH-QUALITY PAPER
IS AVAILABLE FOR THOSE OF YOU
WHO LIKE TO GO
ALL IN
WITH YOUR ART SUPPLIES (LIKE ME)...

CHECK HEYLIVEWIRE.COM
FOR UPDATES AND AVAILABILITY.

THE SPARK

WAKE UP THE WILD.
PLAY WITH THE EDGES.
STIR THE EMBERS.

PHASE 1: DAYS 1 - 30

01

WHAT PART OF YOU HAVE YOU BEEN KEEPING ON A LEASH?

When did you start leashing this part of you?
Who told you it needed to be contained?
What would life look like if you unclipped it?

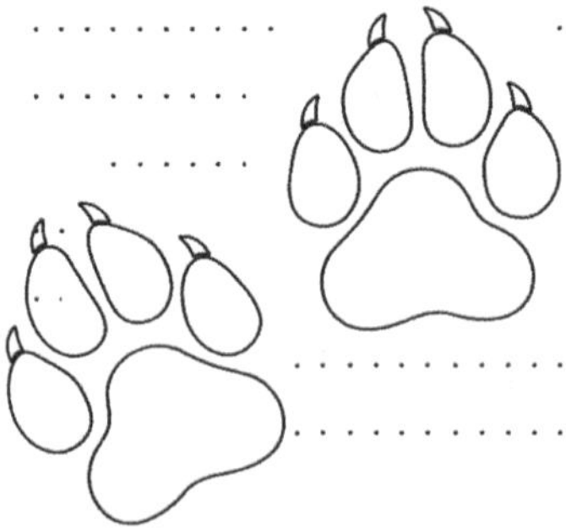

LEASHES ARE FOR DOGS. YOU'RE A DAMN LION.

MINI MEDITATION

Close your eyes. Imagine the leash falling from your hand. The part of you it held takes one cautious step forward, then another... and then bolts, laughing.

02 WHAT'S THE ONE THING YOU'RE DONE APOLOGIZING FOR?

Think of the last time you shrank or said "sorry" for it. Why? What was the truth underneath that moment?

SOME PEOPLE WILL SAY YOU'VE CHANGED. GOOD.

MINI MEDITATION

Picture yourself holding a giant "sorry" balloon.
Let go. Watch it float away until it's gone from sight.

03 WHAT'S ONE SMALL RISK YOU COULD TAKE TODAY – ONE THAT MAKES YOUR STOMACH FLIP?

Write out both the best and worst-case scenarios. Which one's worth living for?

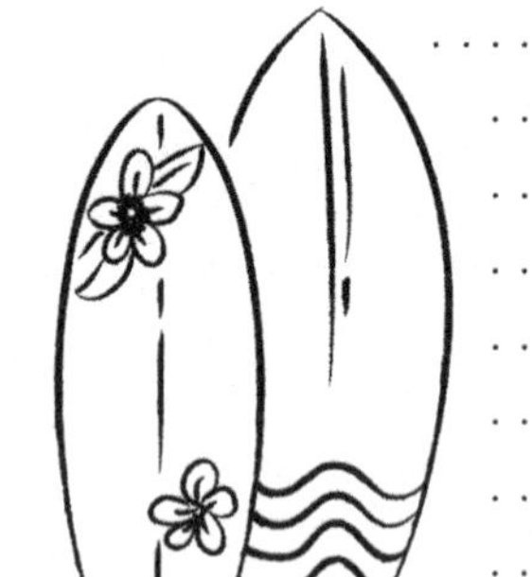

SMALL RISKS LEAD TO BIGGER WAVES.

MINI MEDITATION

You're on the edge of the diving board. Feel your legs coil, ready. Bend. Push. Fly.

04

LIST TEN BRAVE THINGS YOU'VE DONE — BIG OR SMALL.

Choose one and write the moment you decided "yes" instead of "no."

YOU HAVE RECEIPTS FOR YOUR COURAGE.

MINI MEDITATION

Imagine a wall with your name on it, carved beside every brave act you've ever taken. You've been building this all along.

05 IF YOU SPOKE YOUR TRUTH WITH ZERO FEAR OF CONSEQUENCE, WHAT WOULD YOU SAY – AND TO WHOM?

Let the words out on paper. Don't edit. Don't soften.
Just release.

TRUTH FEELS DANGEROUS ONLY WHEN YOU'VE BEEN TAUGHT TO SWALLOW IT.

MINI MEDITATION

Your throat is a river mouth. No dam. No rocks. Just a rush of clear water pouring through.

06

WHAT'S ONE RULE YOU'VE FOLLOWED THAT YOU'RE READY TO BREAK?

Who gave you this rule?
Who benefits if you keep following it?

REBELS MAKE HISTORY. RULE-FOLLOWERS MAKE COPIES.

MINI MEDITATION

Fold the rule into a paper airplane.
Launch it into the sky. Watch it vanish.

07

IF YOU SHOWED UP AT 100% POWER TODAY, WHAT WOULD YOU DO BEFORE SUNDOWN?

Write the day as if it already happened.

YOU WERE BORN TO ELECTRIFY.

MINI MEDITATION

Barefoot on the earth. Lightning splits the sky. Every strike charges you.

08

WHAT'S YOUR FAVORITE SMALL REBELLION?

How does breaking that tiny "rule" make you feel?

SMALL REBELLIONS KEEP THE SOUL LIMBER.

MINI MEDITATION

See yourself stepping over an invisible line... then turning back to wink.

09 WHAT NICKNAME WOULD YOUR INNER WILD CHILD GIVE YOU?

Describe her — your wild child.
What's she wearing? What's her laugh like?

SHE'S BEEN WAITING FOR YOU.

MINI MEDITATION

Picture her taking your hand, pulling you toward the playground gate.

10

WHAT'S A "NO" YOU WISH YOU'D SAID SOONER?

What would have shifted if you had?
What can you say "no" to now?

No!

MINI MEDITATION

Feel the word "no" in your mouth like a perfectly cut diamond.

"IF YOU OBEY ALL THE RULES, YOU MISS ALL THE FUN."

-KATHARINE HEPBURN

You didn't think I'd waste a blank page, did you?

WHAT'S SPARKING IN YOU RIGHT NOW?

11 THE LAST TIME YOU LAUGHED SO HARD YOU SNORTED.

Who were you with? What made you feel so free?

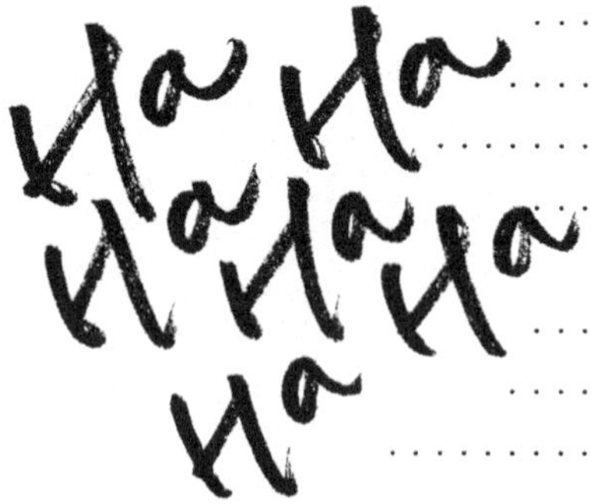

SNORT-LAUGHS ARE SOUL MEDICINE.

MINI MEDITATION

Let your shoulders drop and laugh out loud — right now, even if it's fake.

12 A SKILL YOU LEARNED THE HARD WAY.

What did it cost you? What did it give you?

HARD-EARNED SKILLS HAVE SHARP EDGES — AND YOU KNOW HOW TO USE THEM.

MINI MEDITATION

Imagine holding that skill in your hands like a tool forged in fire.

13 A PIECE OF ADVICE YOU'VE OUTGROWN.

Who gave it to you? How would you rewrite it for yourself now?

MINI MEDITATION

Picture yourself tossing that outdated advice into a bonfire.

14

A COMPLIMENT YOU DIDN'T BELIEVE – BUT SHOULD HAVE.

Why was it hard to take in? What if it was true?

MINI MEDITATION

Imagine yourself breathing the words in like oxygen.

15 YOUR MOST "UNLADYLIKE" VICTORY.

Who told you it was unladylike?
What would you say to them now?

YOU DON'T NEED THEIR ETIQUETTE.

MINI MEDITATION

See yourself planting a flag at the top of that victory.

16

A MOMENT YOU SURPRISED YOURSELF WITH COURAGE.

What sparked the "yes" in you?

YOU'VE DONE BRAVE BEFORE. YOU CAN DO IT AGAIN.

MINI MEDITATION

Stand in that moment again, feeling the heartbeat, the breath.

17

YOUR FAVORITE SCAR – AND THE RIDICULOUS OR BEAUTIFUL STORY BEHIND IT.

Write the scene in detail. Celebrate it.

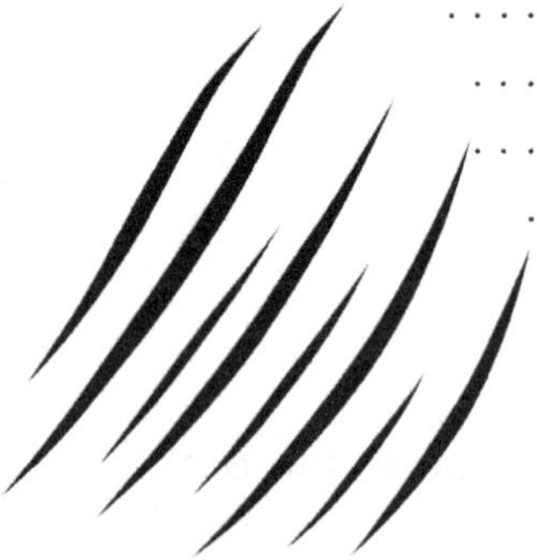

SOME MARKS ARE MEDALS.

MINI MEDITATION

Run your fingers over it, honoring the life it proves you've lived.

18

A DECISION YOU MADE WITHOUT OVERTHINKING.

What happened because you trusted yourself?

QUICK TRUST CAN BE PURE MAGIC.

MINI MEDITATION

Picture that decision as a door you stepped through — and never looked back.

19

SOMETHING YOU ONCE FEARED BUT NOW CRAVE.

How did it transform from fear to desire?

FEAR IS OFTEN THE SEED OF LONGING.

MINI MEDITATION

Let the craving fill your chest like warm light.

20 THE WILDEST THING YOU'VE DONE FOR JOY.

What did it cost? Was it worth it?

MINI MEDITATION

Feel that joy in your body again — where does it live?

"WELL-BEHAVED WOMEN SELDOM MAKE HISTORY."

-LAUREL THATCHER ULRICH

This page won't be blank for long...

USE IT TO JOT DOWN WHAT THIS QUOTE STIRS IN YOU — A THOUGHT, A FEELING, A FLICKER OF SOMETHING TRUE.

21

THE TIME YOU FELT MOST AT HOME IN YOUR SKIN.

Where were you? Who were you with?

MINI MEDITATION

See yourself there again, fully inhabiting your body.

22 ONE THING YOU'D WEAR IF YOU DIDN'T CARE WHAT ANYONE THOUGHT.

How would it make you feel walking down the street in it?

CONFIDENCE IS THE BEST FABRIC.

MINI MEDITATION

Picture the heads turning, not because of the outfit, but because of your energy.

23

A PLACE WHERE YOU FEEL UNSTOPPABLE.

What happens to your energy there?

SOME PLACES ARE ARMOR.

MINI MEDITATION

Imagine standing there now — nothing can reach you.

24 AN INVITATION YOU WISH YOU'D ACCEPTED.

Why didn't you? Would you say yes now?

SOMETIMES THE ANSWER COMES LATER.

MINI MEDITATION

See yourself stepping forward and saying yes.

25 SOMETHING YOU'VE MASTERED THAT NO ONE KNOWS ABOUT.

Why is it a secret? Who would you want to share it with?

MINI MEDITATION

Picture yourself revealing it to someone and watching their eyes light up.

26 THE LAST TIME YOU DANCED YOUR HEART OUT.

What made you let go?

FOOLISH DANCING IS HOLY WORK.

MINI MEDITATION

Let your body move for 20 seconds right now.

27 YOUR MOST BADASS PHOTO.

Where were you?
What was happening around that shot?

MINI MEDITATION

See that moment in slow motion.

28

A SOUND THAT MAKES YOU FEEL POWERFUL.

Why that sound? What does it connect to in you?

MINI MEDITATION

Play it in your mind on repeat.

29

THE ONE THING YOU'D TELL YOUR 20-YEAR-OLD SELF.

How would she react to hearing it?

MINI MEDITATION

Picture her hearing your words and smiling.

30 A WILD DREAM YOU STILL HAVEN'T SAID OUT LOUD.

Write it here. No edits. No excuses.

IT'S TIME SHE HEARD HER OWN DREAM.

MINI MEDITATION

Whisper it. Let it echo inside you.

"You were wild once. Don't let them tame you."

-Isadora Duncan

THE FLAME

TURN UP THE VOLTAGE.
TAKE UP SPACE.
OWN THE HEAT.

PHASE 2: DAYS 31 - 60

31 THE THING YOU WANT MORE OF – AND ARE WILLING TO CLAIM.

Why haven't you claimed it yet?
What changes when you do?

YOU CAN WANT WITHOUT APOLOGY.

MINI MEDITATION

Picture yourself walking into a room and simply taking what's already got your name on it.

32 THE CONVERSATION YOU'VE BEEN AVOIDING.

What's the truth you're afraid will come out?

AVOIDANCE IS A SLOW LEAK. TRUTH IS A CLEAN CUT.

MINI MEDITATION

See yourself speaking it, steady and calm, while the world keeps spinning.

33 A HABIT THAT DIMS YOUR LIGHT – AND WHAT YOU'LL DO INSTEAD.

What's the payoff of keeping the habit?
What's the payoff of dropping it?

YOU GET TO BE LUMINOUS.

MINI MEDITATION

Imagine blowing out a candle... and then relighting it twice as bright.

34 THE LAST TIME YOU SET A BOUNDARY AND MEANT IT.

How did it feel to hold that line?

BOUNDARIES ARE INVITATIONS FOR RESPECT.

MINI MEDITATION

See yourself drawing a clear circle around your space in gold light.

35 YOUR "DON'T MESS WITH ME" FACE.

When was the last time you used it — what effect did it have on others?

YOU CAN SMILE AND STILL MEAN BUSINESS.

MINI MEDITATION

Picture your gaze steady, unblinking, warm with self-assurance.

36

A BELIEF YOU'RE DISMANTLING RIGHT NOW.

Who built it in you? How are you taking it apart?

NOT ALL WALLS PROTECT — SOME JUST BLOCK THE SUN.

MINI MEDITATION

See yourself removing bricks from a wall until the view opens.

37

THE WAY YOUR BODY SAYS "YES" BEFORE YOUR MIND CATCHES UP.

What was the last time you trusted that instinct?

YOUR BODY'S WISDOM RUNS AHEAD OF YOUR THOUGHTS.

MINI MEDITATION

Let your body lean forward slightly — notice where it wants to go.

38

THE BRAVEST WORD YOU'VE SPOKEN THIS YEAR.

What did it cost you? What did it give you?

MINI MEDITATION

Say it out loud again — let it ring in the air.

39

WHAT YOU'D START IF YOU WEREN'T AFRAID TO FAIL.

What would you need to believe to begin anyway?

THE STARTING GUN IS YOURS TO FIRE.

MINI MEDITATION

See yourself at the starting line, heart pounding, feet ready.

40 THE TIME YOU TOOK THE SCENIC (AND REBELLIOUS) ROUTE.

What did you see or learn that you'd have missed otherwise?

THE LONG WAY IS OFTEN THE SOUL'S SHORTCUT.

MINI MEDITATION

Picture winding roads, unexpected views, your hair in the wind.

"FALL SEVEN TIMES AND STAND UP EIGHT."

-JAPANESE PROVERB

Sometimes what doesn't fit on the other pages belongs here.

LET YOUR THOUGHTS SPILL OVER....

41

ONE THING YOU'VE BEEN TOLD IS "TOO MUCH" THAT'S ACTUALLY PERFECT.

How would you live if you believed it was exactly right?

MINI MEDITATION

Imagine turning the volume up on that trait until it fills the room.

42

THE WAY YOU'D CELEBRATE IF YOU DIDN'T HOLD BACK.

What's stopping you from celebrating like that now?

MINI MEDITATION

See yourself dancing, shouting, or toasting without glancing around for approval.

43

SOMETHING YOU'RE BUILDING QUIETLY, WITHOUT ANNOUNCING.

Why keep it quiet? How will you know it's ready to show?

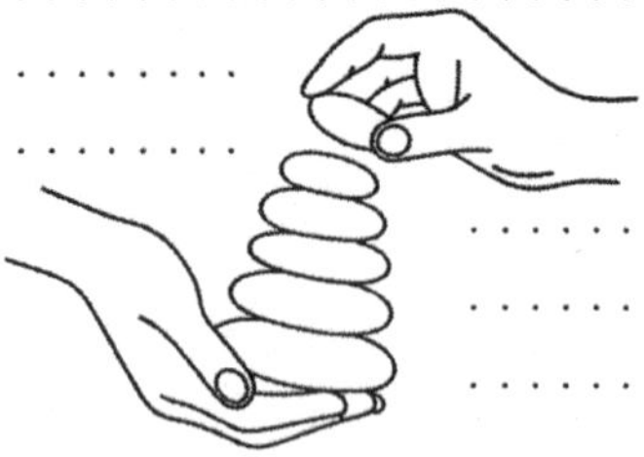

NOT ALL POWER NEEDS AN AUDIENCE.

MINI MEDITATION

Picture it glowing softly, growing stronger every day without needing eyes on it.

44

YOUR PROUDEST UNPLANNED MOMENT.

What made it so right in the moment?

SOME VICTORIES AREN'T ON THE TO-DO LIST.

MINI MEDITATION

See yourself making the choice on instinct — and smiling after.

45 WHAT YOU'D PAINT ON THE SIDE OF A BUILDING IF YOU COULD.

Why that? What message are you sending to strangers?

MINI MEDITATION

Imagine the mural 30 feet high, your colors blazing in the sun.

46 A TIME YOU LED WITHOUT REALIZING IT.

Who followed you? What did you model for them?

LEADERSHIP OFTEN HAPPENS SIDEWAYS.

MINI MEDITATION

See them walking beside you now, because you lit the way.

47

THE SONG YOU'D WALK INTO A ROOM TO.

How does it feel in your body as the first notes hit?

EVERY QUEEN NEEDS AN ENTRANCE THEME.

MINI MEDITATION

Play the song in your head. Walk into your next room with that rhythm in your step.

48

A RISK YOU'D TAKE IF YOU TRUSTED YOURSELF MORE.

What's one step toward that risk you could take today?

SELF-TRUST IS THE ONLY PERMISSION SLIP YOU NEED.

MINI MEDITATION

See yourself holding your own hand as you step over the threshold.

49 A "HELL YES" YOU'RE GLAD YOU SAID.

How has that yes shaped you?

HELL YES AGES WELL.

MINI MEDITATION

Relive that yes — the moment before, the leap, the landing.

50 THE WILD PLACE YOU STILL WANT TO VISIT.

What would you do there that you can't do anywhere else?

SOME PLACES ARE WAITING JUST FOR YOU.

MINI MEDITATION

Picture the first breath you'll take when you arrive.

"YOU WILL NEVER INFLUENCE THE WORLD BY TRYING TO BE LIKE IT."

-UNKNOWN

Every spark, every flame needs space to breathe.

PAUSE HERE. BREATHE.
SCRIBBLE WHATEVER'S ALIVE IN THIS MOMENT.

51

YOUR FAVORITE PHYSICAL EXPRESSION OF POWER.

What does your body know about strength?

MINI MEDITATION

Stand, stretch, feel the strength in your bones.

52 A RULE YOU INVENTED FOR YOURSELF – AND LOVE.

Why does it work for you? How can you lean into it more?

MINI MEDITATION

Write the rule on an imaginary banner and hang it over your life.

53

THE LAST TIME YOU CAUGHT YOUR REFLECTION & LIKED IT.

What exactly did you see in that moment?

SHE'S STILL IN THERE.

MINI MEDITATION

Look in a mirror now. Find that same angle, that same light.

54 THE TIME YOU REFUSED TO SETTLE.

What was the price of not settling? What was the reward?

REFUSAL IS AN ACT OF SELF-RESPECT.

MINI MEDITATION

Picture yourself walking away from "good enough" toward "right for me."

55 ONE "IMPOSSIBLE" THING YOU'VE DONE.

What made it possible?

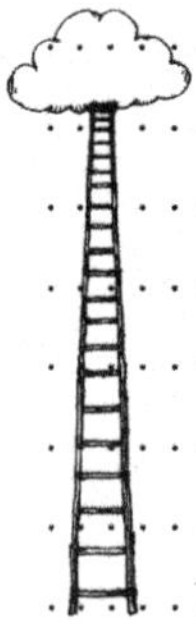

MINI MEDITATION

See yourself standing at the edge, knowing it can be done because you did it.

56 A BOLD COLOR THAT FEELS LIKE YOU.

What does that color say about you?

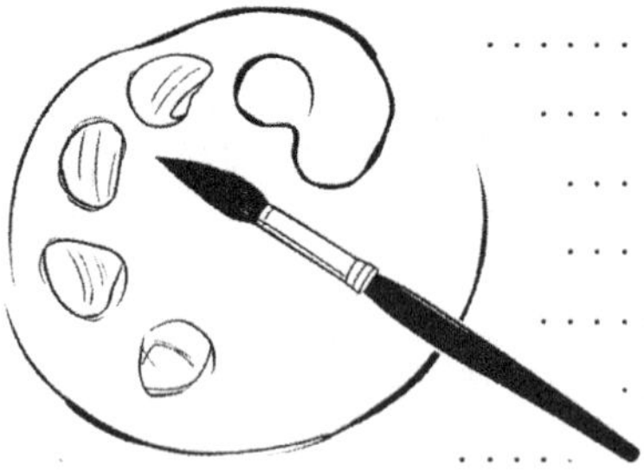

COLOR IS MOOD IN PIGMENT FORM.

MINI MEDITATION

Wrap yourself in that color until you glow with it.

57

YOUR MOST REBELLIOUS ACT OF SELF-CARE.

Why was it rebellious?

SELF-CARE CAN BE A PROTEST.

MINI MEDITATION

Picture yourself doing it again — but louder.

58 A TRUTH YOU'RE FINALLY READY TO NAME.

What changes when you name it out loud?

TRUTH IS AN AMPLIFIER.

MINI MEDITATION

Say it quietly first, then louder, until your whole body hears.

59

THE THING YOU'D DO IF NO ONE COULD STOP YOU.

What's one step toward it you can take today?

UNSTOPPABLE IS A MUSCLE YOU BUILD.

MINI MEDITATION

Picture the first motion toward it — and just begin.

60

THE MOMENT YOU REALIZED YOU WERE UNSTOPPABLE.

What was the spark? What did you do with it?

YOU'VE BEEN THE FORCE ALL ALONG.

MINI MEDITATION

Stand tall. Feel that same power settle back into your bones.

"ABOVE ALL; BE THE HEROINE OF YOUR LIFE, NOT THE VICTIM."

-NORA EPHRON

THE STORM

STAND IN YOUR FULL
UNAPOLOGETIC SELF.
BE THE LIGHTNING.

PHASE 3: DAYS 61 - 90

61

THE STORM YOU'VE ALREADY WEATHERED – AND WHAT IT MADE YOU.

How are you stronger because of it?

THE STORM WAS NEVER BIGGER THAN YOU.

MINI MEDITATION

Stand in the rain, feel it wash the dust from your skin. You are clean, unbroken, unbowed.

62 THE MOST DANGEROUS THING ABOUT YOU (IN THE BEST WAY).

How does this "danger" serve you and the people you love?

YOUR POWER ISN'T A THREAT — IT'S A BEACON.

MINI MEDITATION

Hold that danger like a lit torch. See the way it lights the dark.

THE MOMENT YOU KNEW YOU WERE DONE PLAYING SMALL.

What happened in your body when you decided?

SMALL WAS NEVER YOUR SIZE.

MINI MEDITATION

Picture your shoulders rolling back, your breath deepening — your size returning.

THE CHOICE THAT CHANGED EVERYTHING.

What if you hadn't made it?

CHOICE IS THE BIRTHPLACE OF DESTINY.

MINI MEDITATION

See the fork in the road, one path dusty, one path alive with color. You chose the color.

65

THE WAY YOU MOVE WHEN YOU'RE UNAFRAID.

How can you move like that today?

FEARLESS HAS A POSTURE.

MINI MEDITATION

Stand tall. Feel that same power settle back into your bones.

66

YOUR FAVORITE PROOF THAT YOU'RE ALIVE.

What senses fire up in that moment?

PROOF OF LIFE IS IN THE LIVING.

MINI MEDITATION

Feel the air in your lungs, the pulse in your wrists. You're here.

67

THE HILL YOU'RE WILLING TO DIE ON.

Why does it matter that much?

SOME HILLS ARE WORTH THE CLIMB.

MINI MEDITATION

Stand on that hill in your mind, the wind whipping your hair, your stance unshakable.

68

THE LEGACY YOU'RE BUILDING RIGHT NOW.

Who will feel the ripple of your work?

YOUR FUTURE IS ALREADY IN MOTION.

MINI MEDITATION

Picture the ripple spreading wider and wider across a still lake.

69

A MOMENT THAT STILL GIVES YOU GOOSEBUMPS.

Where does it live in your body?

GOOSEBUMPS ARE THE BODY'S APPLAUSE.

MINI MEDITATION

Close your eyes and let the shiver rise again.

70 THE TIME YOU TOOK CONTROL OF THE WHEEL.

What were you steering away from — and toward?

MINI MEDITATION

Feel your hands on the wheel, your eyes locked on the horizon.

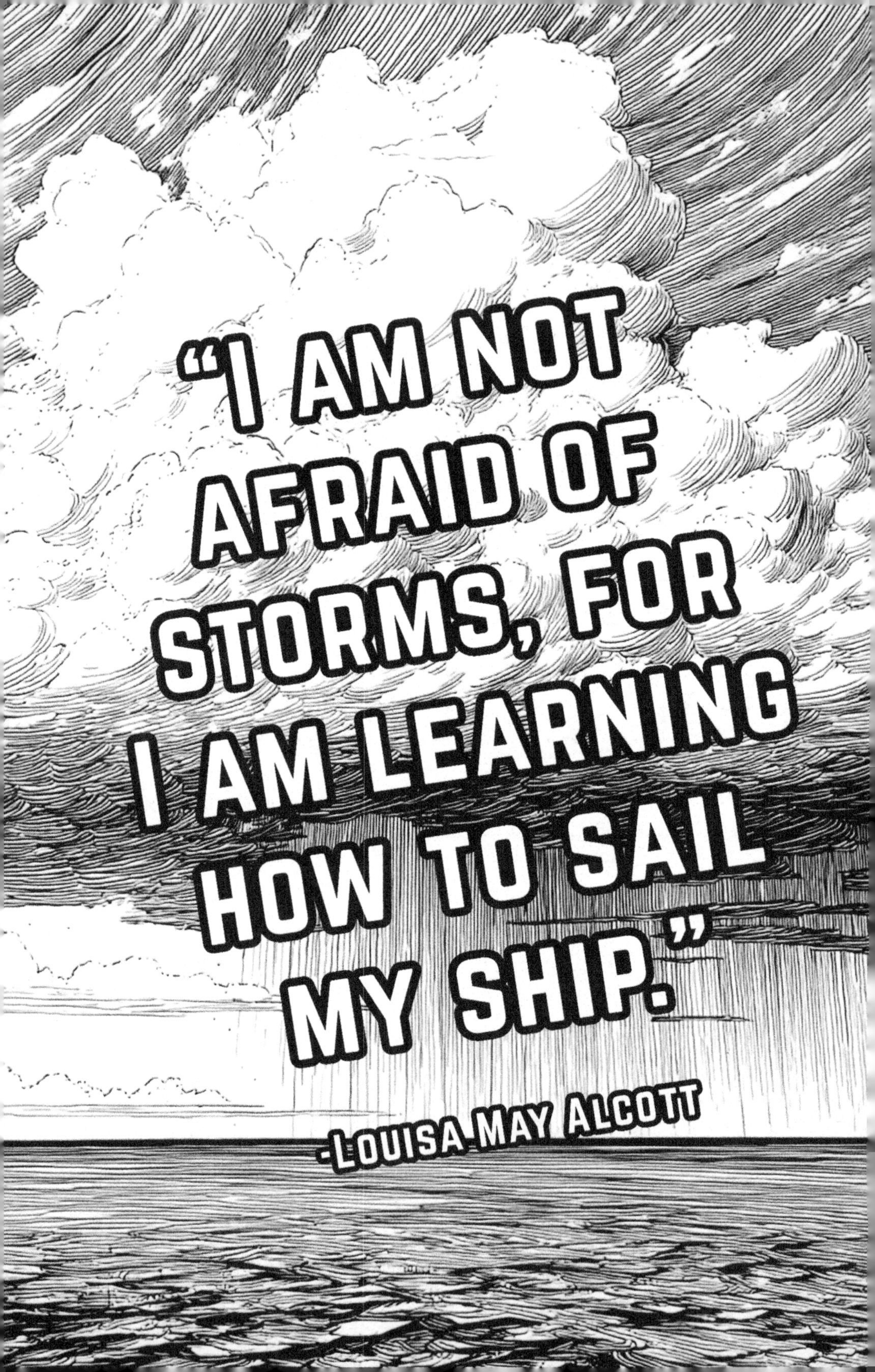
"I AM NOT AFRAID OF STORMS, FOR I AM LEARNING HOW TO SAIL MY SHIP."
-LOUISA MAY ALCOTT

Energy doesn't stop at the edge of the page.

KEEP GOING. CAPTURE WHAT'S STILL HUMMING UNDERNEATH.

71 THE LOUDEST "YES" YOUR SOUL HAS EVER SHOUTED.

What did it open for you?

MINI MEDITATION

Hear it echo back to you, like mountains answering mountains.

72 YOUR MOST DEFIANT SMILE.

Who was it for? Or against?

A SMILE CAN BE ARMOR.

MINI MEDITATION

See that smile in the mirror. Wear it for the rest of the day.

73

THE WAY YOU LIGHT UP A ROOM WITHOUT TRYING.

What's your secret ingredient?

YOU DON'T HAVE TO TRY — YOU JUST HAVE TO BE.

MINI MEDITATION

Picture the glow leaving you like sunlight spilling across the floor.

74

A FEAR YOU'VE OUTLIVED.

How did you outgrow it?

IT DOESN'T FIT ANYMORE.

MINI MEDITATION

See that fear as a pair of shoes two sizes too small. Take them off.

75

THE LAST TIME YOU DIDN'T WAIT YOUR TURN.

What did you gain by stepping forward?

YOUR TURN IS NOW.

MINI MEDITATION

Walk to the front of the line in your mind.
Take the seat you want.

A TIME YOU SAVED YOURSELF.

What did you learn about your own strength?

YOU'VE BEEN YOUR OWN HERO ALL ALONG.

MINI MEDITATION

Place your hand over your heart. Feel the steady beat that was always yours.

77

THE THING YOU'RE WILLING TO FIGHT FOR EVERY DAY.

Why does it deserve your energy?

SOME BATTLES ARE WORTH THE BRUISES.

MINI MEDITATION

See yourself sharpening your tools, ready to step into the arena.

THE SOUND OF YOUR OWN POWER.

How would you describe it?

POWER HAS ITS OWN FREQUENCY.

MINI MEDITATION

Hear it — whether it's a roar, a hum, or the crackle before thunder.

79

YOUR PROUDEST BATTLE SCAR – THE MARK THAT SAYS, "I FOUGHT FOR THIS & I'D DO IT AGAIN."

What was the fight, and why was it worth it?

YOU BLED, YOU HEALED, YOU ROSE.

MINI MEDITATION

Run your hand over the scar, honoring the story it tells.

80 THE MOMENT YOU BECAME THE STORM.

What did it feel like in your body?

MINI MEDITATION

See yourself as the wind, the rain, the lightning — unstoppable.

"COURAGE IS LIKE A MUSCLE. WE STRENGTHEN IT BY USE."

-MIA HAMM

This one's yours.

DRAW, DOODLE, OR WRITE SOMETHING THAT REMINDS YOU YOU'RE ALIVE.

81

THE TRUTH THAT COULD START A REVOLUTION.

What would change if you spoke it?

MINI MEDITATION

Stand in a crowded square in your mind and speak it into the air.

82 THE WAY YOU LOVE WHEN YOU'RE FEARLESS.

What's different about you then?

FEARLESS LOVE IS FREEDOM.

MINI MEDITATION

See yourself loving without guardrails, arms wide.

83

THE TIME YOU MADE SOMEONE BELIEVE IN THEMSELVES.

What did you say or do that lit them up?

YOU'VE BEEN SOMEONE'S TURNING POINT.

MINI MEDITATION

See their face, feel the warmth in your chest.

84 THE LOUDEST "NO" YOU'VE EVER SAID.

What door did that close — and what one did it open?

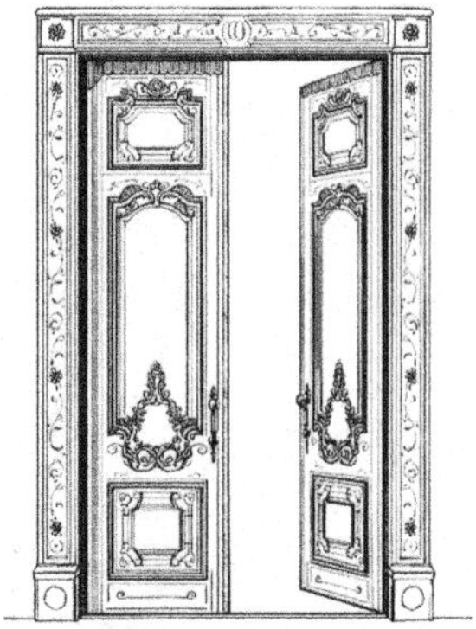

NO IS A KIND OF LIBERATION.

MINI MEDITATION

Feel the weight lift as the "no" leaves your lips.

THE DREAM YOU'RE NOW LIVING.

When did you realize it was here?

MINI MEDITATION

Look around your real life for proof — and thank it.

86

A MOMENT YOU'LL CARRY INTO THE NEXT LIFETIME.

Why does it deserve eternity?

SOME MOMENTS ARE FOREVER.

MINI MEDITATION

Place it gently into a golden box in your mind.

87

THE PERSON YOU'VE BECOME DESPITE THE ODDS.

Who tried to stop you? How did you keep going?

ODDS DON'T GET TO DECIDE.

MINI MEDITATION

See yourself walking past every obstacle, eyes fixed ahead.

88

THE TIME YOU STARED DOWN THE WAVE AND PADDLED IN ANYWAY.

What was waiting on the other side?

FEAR IS JUST THE FIRST RIPPLE.

MINI MEDITATION

Feel the drop, the rush, the ride.

89

THE WILDEST THING ABOUT YOUR FUTURE SELF.

How can you bring a piece of her into today?

YOUR FUTURE IS ALREADY SHOWING UP.

MINI MEDITATION

See her standing in front of you. Take one thing from her and make it yours now.

90

THE STORM INSIDE YOU – AND THE CALM YOU CARRY WITH IT.

How do you balance both?

YOU ARE THE EYE AND THE HURRICANE.

MINI MEDITATION

Feel the lightning and the stillness living in the same breath.

"SHE REMEMBERED WHO SHE WAS, AND THE GAME CHANGED."

-LALAH DELIA

You've done something extraordinary — you showed up for yourself, day after day.

The sparks you've gathered here will keep lighting your way forward. Keep going. Keep glowing.

You're a LIVE WIRE!

AND REMEMBER, EVERY ENDING HUMS WITH THE NEXT BEGINNING...

YOU'VE FACED THE WAVES.
YOU'VE BROKEN THE RULES. YOU'VE WALKED STRAIGHT INTO THE STORM

—

AND YOU'RE STILL STANDING.

The ***Live Wire Journal*** is 90 days of unapologetic prompts, grit-laced reflections, and lightning-strike meditations to wake up your wild and keep you buzzing.

From spark to flame to full-blown storm, each page dares you to take up space, tell the truth, and stop apologizing for the power in your bones.

YOU ARE NOT HERE TO BE SMALL.
YOU ARE HERE TO ELECTRIFY.

SPARK, FLAME, STORM

Made in the USA
Monee, IL
12 December 2025

36223479R00115